THE HEALING POWER OF THE FAMILY:

An Illustrated Overview of Life with the Disturbed Foster or Adopted Child

2nd Edition

Richard J. Delaney, Ph.D.

Illustrated by Terry McNerney

To my wife and children
and to their own special healing power.

Published by:

Wood 'N' Barnes Publishing
2717 NW 50th Street
Oklahoma City, OK 73112
(405) 946-0621

2nd Edition copyright 1997, Wood 'N' Barnes Publishing
All rights reserved.

Original copyright property of Richard J. Delaney, Ph. D.

Printed in the United States of America
Oklahoma City, Oklahoma
ISBN # 1-885473-16-8

To order copies of Dr. Delaney's
books, please call:
Jean Barnes Books
800-678-0621

About the Author

Dr. Rick Delaney is a nationally-known consultant and trainer. He is a clinical psychologist with a private practice in Ft. Collins, Colorado. Specializing in work with foster and adoptive children, he is a consultant to the Casey Family Program, Lutheran Family Services and to county departments of social services. He works closely with foster and adoptive parent support groups.

Dr. Delaney is the author of:
Fostering Changes: Treating Attachment-Disordered Foster Children;
Troubled Transplants: Unconventional Strategies for Helping Disturbed Foster and Adopted Children (with co-author, Dr. Frank R. Kunstal); and
Long Journey Home (an illustrated children's book with drawings by Terry McNerney).
Raising Cain: Caring for Troubled Youngsters/Repairing Our Troubled System

Dr. Delaney is available for consultation, seminars and training sessions.

To schedule these events you may make your initial contact through his publisher:

**Wood 'N' Barnes
Publishing
(800) 678-0621**

TABLE OF CONTENTS

PREFACE

After six months of foster care work, one emotionally exhausted foster mother commented, only half-jokingly, "My one regret in life is that I wasn't someone else."

An adoptive father, concerned about his wife's depression related to parenting, remarked wistfully, "Before we adopted Jamie (age eight) last year, we were a happily married couple."

A single foster/adoptive father, after two tumultuous years with Bobby (ten years old), commented, "The belief is, 'Every child deserves a family.' But, I ask, 'What family deserves this child?'"

Parents willing to provide foster care or an adoptive home to formerly abused children are an endangered species. In the early 1980's, foster parents numbered 150,000. However, by the 1990's their rank has shrunk to 100,000. Why such sharp drop off? Why such dramatic attrition?

In great part the precipitous decline in willing families relates to the severity of children's emotional and behavioral problems coming into care. In the case of a foster mother whose nose was broken during a young child's temper tantrum; or in the adoptive family wherein the mother received broken ribs from a violent kick by her adopted son; or in the home of a single foster father where false allegations of sexual abuse by his teenaged foster son cost the unfortunate man his job--in each incident the parent figures have become victims of the child's disturbance.

According to Paul Steinhauer, M.D., the healthy family offers the child a nurturing "cradle of development". However, in the case of chronic maltreatment, the child is raised in a nest of thorns. Growing up in the thorny, hostile home life, the child expects the worst from caregivers. His or her negative expectations may continue long after the child has been removed from the source of maltreatment. Even in the protective, loving foster or adoptive family, the child's suspicion, anger and anxiety about past caregivers, persist. Locked in the past, the child may unwittingly recreate by his negative expectations and corresponding behavior an adoptive or foster family which resembles his earlier, maltreating family. With that, foster or adoptive parents become "prisoners of deja vu", reluctantly drawn into a reenactment of the child's sad history.

A second factor in the decline of willing foster and adoptive parents is that of inadequate preparation and follow-up support to the parents. Specifically, these parents remain insufficiently informed of the significant behavioral and emotional challenges which the formerly maltreated child will present in care. Likewise, they are poorly prepared for the extensive changes in family dynamics which often follow the child's placement in their home. Lastly, foster and adoptive parents with disturbed children are rarely equipped with therapeutic strategies for dealing with the emotional tumult and problem behaviors which accompany troubled children.

The Healing Power of the Family addresses several areas of vital importance for those parents who live with disturbed foster and adopted children and for those professionals who train, support and collaborate with these parents and the children.

This book has grown out of workshops I have presented in the United States and Canada over the past four years. These workshops have underscored the central importance of the foster or adoptive family in turning around the lives of significantly troubled children and youth. They have also focused upon the curative relationships within the foster or adoptive family setting which can alter the child's cynical expectations about himself, caregivers and the world in general. The premise here is that emotional and sometimes physical wounds suffered by children during their unfortunate pasts may often respond dramatically to the healing power of the family--foster or adoptive. Moreover, proper understanding and preparation can magnify the positive influence of the family upon the child and diminish the negative impact of the child's disturbance on the family.

(NOTE: to safeguard the privacy and confidentiality of children and families, the cases and examples used herein have been fictionalized and disguised or are psychological composites. Any resemblance to actual specific individuals or families is due to the sad fact that the traumatic histories and symptoms of maltreated children often form a common, familiar mosaic.)

Richard J. Delaney   Fort Collins, Colorado August, 1995

OVERVIEW OF THE BOOK

*T*he *Healing Power of the Family* offers a nontechnical, user-friendly approach to the understanding and treatment of disturbed foster and adopted children. (For theoretical background the reader is referred to the references/recommended reading section ahead.) It presents in written and graphic form the concepts presented in my workshops for foster and adoptive parents, group and residential home staff, hospital personnel, teachers, and mental health and agency staff. This book also includes numerous visual illustrations which have been shown at the workshops by means of photographic slides. These illustrations are impactful, often lighthearted drawings by Terry McNerney, illustrator of the children's book, *The Long Journey Home.*

Chapter One (with accompanying illustrations) addresses the staggering statistics related to increases in foster care placements and to the upsurge in the numbers of disturbed children in foster and special need's adoptive homes.

Chapter Two enumerates the most common behavioral/emotional problems observed in children who have been formerly maltreated and later reside in foster or adoptive families.

Chapter Three describes the disturbed child's powerfully negative impact on the foster or adoptive parents.

Chapter Four discusses ten examples of family-based interventions which have been employed by families in helping their troubled foster or adopted children. These examples are provided not as "cookbook" recipes for helping individual children but as illustrations of the creativity and ingenuity which is frequently required by teams of individuals (e.g. foster parents, therapists, and agency workers) to curb acting-out behaviors and foster attachments with disturbed children.

Lastly, **Chapter Five** addresses four special issues related to foster and adopted children: the phenomenon of idealization and devaluation of parent figures; the search for biological roots; triggers which set off loss-sensitive children; and finally, the concept of resiliency or invulnerability in maltreated children.

ACKNOWLEDGMENTS

I would like to express my gratitude to Marqueena Cleaver and Judy Browning for their painstaking proofreading of this work.

For critical comments about the concepts in this book, I am most thankful to Vera Fahlberg, M.D.

And lastly, to those foster and adoptive parents who have provided me with their great insights into the vicissitudes of living with and loving troubled children, I am most appreciative.

CHAPTER ONE: Introduction _____

The size of the child maltreatment problem in the United States and Canada is both mind-boggling and mind-numbing. X number of children physically abused per year, Y number of youngsters sexually abused each day, Z number of youth understimulated, undernourished, underloved per minute. In its statistical format, hard, cold research appears devoid of humanity. While data on child maltreatment presents us with the magnitude of the problem, numerical abstractions fail to accurately depict the toll child abuse, neglect, and sexual exploitation have taken on the lives of individual children. Thus, we are left with a sense of unreality.

Of course, to individual victims of abuse and to those who care for those injured children in foster or adoptive homes, child abuse is no statistical abstraction. It's as real as it gets.

Before turning to the realities of living with, loving and working with formerly abused foster and adopted children, we first turn to relevant statistics about increases in placement of children and then to a more philosophical discussion about what "the system" does to hurt the children it would like to help.

"When it comes to the placement of older foster and adopted children, we find an overworked stork..."

The Overworked Stork

As a nation, we face a crisis in our beleaguered child welfare system. That system has been increasingly inundated by a flood of abused, neglected and exploited children into foster and adoptive care. The statistics about out-of-home placements are daunting: in 1980 there were approximately 250,000 children living in placement; by 1994, there were an estimated 400,000. In the adoption arena, 70,000 special needs children currently await adoptive families.

The burgeoning number of children in out-of-home care reside in foster homes, group homes, residential child care facilities, and psychiatric treatment centers and hospitals. Many of these children languish for years in emotional limbo while the system--both legal and welfare--decides on their futures and permanency. Many children are never adopted, remaining wards of the state, until they are out of the system.

Yearly, the North American Council on Adoptable Children reports the sobering statistics about the enormous number of older children who wait for adoptive families. Many prospective adoptive (and foster) parents are reluctant to commit to the placement of older children, given the common histories of emotional/behavioral problems and past placement disruptions. Thus, when it comes to the placement of older foster and adopted children, we often find an overworked stork in a holding pattern.

"These youngsters are...'Humpty Dumpty' children who are patched together after the fall from the wall..."

The System's Disturbed Children

The past two decades have witnessed an upsurge of disturbed children entering the child welfare system. Veteran foster parents, experienced caseworkers and seasoned therapists unanimously agree that children in the system are alarmingly troubled and traumatized by the time they are placed in out-of-home care.

The reasons for the worsening of children's problems are many; however, the chief causes seem to be:

> 1) the legacy of years of underfunding of programs for families and children;
>
> 2) the inability of the legal and welfare system to cope with the massive numbers of children and families identified;
>
> 3) the increase in drug and alcohol-affected babies and children;
>
> 4) injudicious attempts at keeping "untreatable" families together, e.g. through family preservation; and
>
> 5) premature or poorly developed efforts at putting unprepared families and children back together, e.g. through family reunification.

These youngsters are, in effect, "Humpty Dumpty" children who are patched together after the fall from the wall only to be inadvisably and repeatedly replaced on the wall again. These fractured children time and again suffer abuse, neglect and/or sexual exploitation along with the confusion and trauma of repeated moves. In time, all the King's horses and helping professionals cannot put these Humpty Dumpty children back together again.

Family preservation and family reunification programs are, in concept, wonderful notions with which few in this field will argue. In practice, however, one sees an increase in children's lives shattered and broken when they remain too long in dangerous, untenable families or when they are returned ill-advisedly to such families.

"With expedited decisions perhaps the Court will cease placing children out on a limb and leaving them there."

Children Out on a Limb

The court system, painstakingly pitting the rights of birth parents against the best interests of maltreated children, often delays decision-making with psychologically inhumane impact upon youngsters. Especially disastrous are protracted court battles in maltreatment cases involving infants and very young children. The inability or reluctance of the court system to act expeditiously to terminate parental rights of untreatable parents leaves children of tender age in limbo. Moreover, the impermanence and sometimes transience which accompanies the "child in limbo" assault the child's emotional stability and his/her capacity to attach to caregivers. The younger the child, the more damaging is the injury to the child's psychological health. With this in mind some state legislatures have enacted laws which expedite the process of decision-making, particularly when children are in their tender years when attachments are so vital to future mental health. With expedited decisions perhaps the Court will cease placing children out on a limb and leaving them there.

"Dysfunctional patterns of interactions and telltale behavior problems are related to what the child has learned from the world of maltreatment which he has observed firsthand."

CHAPTER TWO: Behavior Problems in Troubled Foster or Adopted Children _____

The formerly maltreated foster or adopted child often enters his new family with a number of emotional scars, problematic behaviors and dysfunctional patterns of interaction which seem quite out of place. With three square meals, a roof over his head and all the love and protection he could want, why does the foster or adopted child act out?

It is an understatement to mention that fire-setting, lying, stealing, sexual obsessions and compulsions, and other problematic behaviors do not build emotional bridges between the child and his foster or adoptive family. In fact, these behaviors often destroy tenuous connections between the child and his new family--the family that would like to offer him love and affection. Why, then, do troubled foster and adoptive children stubbornly cling to destructive behaviors?

Mystifying behavior problems make sense if they are seen as an outgrowth of how the child perceives his world, himself and caregivers. The child's expectations or "mental blueprint" of the world inform him that caregivers are dangerous, unreliable and unresponsive. Further, it tells him that he himself is worthless, ineffective and unsafe with or around caregivers. Dysfunctional patterns of interactions and telltale behavior problems are related to what the child has learned from the world of maltreatment which he has observed firsthand. What he or she has learned lingers in his expectations or mental blueprint of the world.

Chapter Two describes nineteen common behavior problems (or symptoms) of the troubled foster or adopted child: cruelty to animals, fire-setting, weak conscience development, enuresis/encopresis, sexualized behavior, vandalism and destruction of property, lying, stealing, low self-esteem/depression, hyperkinesis, insecurities/fears, insatiable neediness, oppositional defiance and stubbornness, explosive temper/tantruming behavior, paranoia/mistrust, runaway behavior, false self/ "as-if" personality, assaultive behavior, and emotional promiscuity. Each behavior problem is depicted by an illustration and explained by an accompanying text.

"In some ways animals make perfect victims."

1. Cruelty to Animals

Cruelty to animals is often symptomatic of underlying anger at the world, and especially at historically maltreating caregivers. Cruelty to animals typically is a form of displacement which can be traced to the child's earliest, most dysfunctional relationships. The rage-filled child may find targeting animals to be a safe outlet for anger he is loathe to express toward a frightening adult world. In some foster and adoptive homes, pets are the undeserving recipients of harassment, torture and even capital punishment.

Cruelty to animals may indicate that the child has witnessed similar behaviors towards himself, other children, his mother or toward animals. One child witnessed the father kick the family cat to death. Many children have observed violent acts toward their mothers. Still others have been the direct recipients of horrendously cruel, harsh and vicious parenting.

In some ways animals make perfect victims. The child can set fire to the dog, feed glass shards to the guinea pig or drown the family cat without repercussion, if he can manufacture clever enough explanations or excuses for what happened. Even if the family does suspect the child, the pet--if still alive--is a poor witness, the perfect victim whose lack of speech renders him somewhat defenseless.

"Fire-setting behavior can sometimes literally burn-out a foster or adoptive home placement very quickly."

2. Fire-Setting

Chronically maltreated children often have a fetish for fire: starting fires, watching fires and reporting fires. Fire is symbolic of the smoldering rage many of these youngsters feel about their tragic upbringing. The pyromaniacal thrill inherent in the act may vent some of the underlying rage within the child.

At times fire-setting may be associated with nothing more sinister than weak impulse control and poor judgment. However, in other instances, it may be a manifestation of attachment problems and sociopathic tendencies. As a sociopathic behavior, fire-setting may be seen when the child feels vengeful. For example, the youngster might incinerate a rival's favorite plaything. Similarly, he might gleefully burn down the foster father's woodshop if he has disciplined him for something. Ironically, he might set fires when he finds himself growing too "warmly" attached or comfortable in the foster or adoptive home.

Not surprisingly, fire-setting behavior can sometimes literally burn-out a foster or adoptive home placement very quickly. Families should carefully inquire before accepting a child into their home about any history of fire-setting.

"In some instances, it's easier to feel like a 'Big Cheese', if you have a Swiss cheese superego."

3. Weak Conscience Development

One oft-reported behavioral problem in maltreated children is the lack of conscience. Children who have been chronically abused are frequently described as "children without conscience", those who do not experience guilt feelings. It is a common observation for foster and adoptive parents that when disturbed children are caught doing something wrong, they feel regret but not remorse. That is, they regret having been caught, but seem to feel no sense of wrongdoing, no compassion for the victim of their misdeeds, and no sense of shame in disappointing their parent figures.

The term, "Swiss Cheese Superego", has been used to describe children who have lacunae or gaps in their conscience formation. These children may be able to verbalize what is right and what is wrong. That is, they can distinguish right from wrong. However, they fail to abide by society's rules or by family values. They stand above the rules, or more accurately, they oftentimes make their own set of rules and develop a moralistic superiority complex. Their underdeveloped conscience, riddled with gaping holes, reinforces a sense of superiority. In some instances, it's easier to feel like a "Big Cheese", if you have a Swiss cheese superego.

Particularly in children who have attachment disorders, we will see a range of conscience or superego deficits. The child who has a faulty or nonexistent attachment towards caregivers, by definition has no intrinsic motivation to learn moral behavior or to attempt to please the adults with good behavior. Thus, the child without healthy attachments does not internalize the rules, values and morals of his/her parent figures. Or, if he/she does, the internalization is incomplete or spotty.

"One angry child urinated on the family pets as they slept. Needless to say, he was not popular with the animals."

4. Enuresis and Encopresis

Many disturbed children, especially those who have been maltreated historically, act out their emotional problems through misuse of bodily waste: urine and feces. Interestingly, with many of these children toilet-training has been a historic battleground. Disturbed youngsters have often revealed to foster parents, adoptive parents, caseworkers and therapists cruel treatment and bizarre parenting behaviors they have received related to toileting issues. One boy, for example, spoke of being tied to the toilet in a darkened bathroom until he would defecate. Other children have had their faces rubbed in any messes they have made. Interestingly, abusive birth parents themselves have often revealed the sometimes harsh and bizarre parenting practices which they felt were appropriate in toilet training their children, e.g. bragging about how they had toilet-trained a child with threats of paddling at the age of nine months.

In a world which the child has come to view as a totalitarian dictatorship, there are very few outlets for self-direction. That is, there exists an atmosphere heavy with parental control. In this world the child has little, if any, say-so in decision-making. Bedwetting, daytime enuresis and encopresis may become convenient, if unpleasant, avenues for expressing the desire for some modicum of control. These unappetizing behavior problems may also serve to express unverbalized anger.

Foster and adoptive parents frequently describe children who urinate in closets, on the carpet, down heat ducts or in the clothes' drawer. One angry child urinated on the family pets as they slept. Needless to say, he was not popular with the animals. While many less troubled children wet their own beds, the disturbed foster and adoptive child may wet other's beds. One insightful psychologist called this "pissive-aggressive" behavior.

Soiling of underwear, smearing of fecal matter and hiding of stained underclothes send loud, if cryptic, messages from the child about the need for control and/or underlying anger at the world. It is the rare parent who is not affected by such uninviting behavior and is not drawn into power struggles over it.

*"One foster father described an eight-year-old foster daughter as a
'Lolita on Hot Wheels'."*

5. Sexualized Behavior

75% to 85% of children placed in out-of-home care have been sexually exploited previously in their lives. These victims of sexual abuse often display a great deal of confusion, guilt and preoccupation with sexual matters. Many foster and adoptive children have been victimized chronically and view themselves as sex objects. They may have developed an expectation that they will be victimized sooner or later by others. Consequently, they perceive themselves as victims and may, ironically, promote victimization by others through seductive behavior or by their unnaturally strong desire to please others. Many sexual abuse victims have an uncanny way of gravitating towards those who would use and abuse them sexually.

Some children who have been sexually abused, at some point begin to exploit others. They become precocious perpetrators, sexually acting-out with other children and sometimes even with animals. Their bizarre histories of sexual exposure often come out in cruel and perverse sexual behaviors toward others. Sexual behaviors can become fused with affectionate feelings or with angry and hostile sentiments toward those around them.

The foster or adoptive parent and worker/therapist who lives with or treats the sexually abused child, often is appalled by the eroticized behavior which even very tiny children may display. Very upsetting to the adult are sexual overtures the child may make toward them. One foster father described an eight-year-old foster daughter as a "Lolita on Hot Wheels"--a sexualized girl who was eight-going-on-twenty-eight. These overtures can be frightening and threatening to the adult, who may prematurely assume that removal of the child from the home is the only way to deal with the problem. There are, however, helpful interventions with sexually abused children which can assist them in learning appropriate ways to interact with adults and children.

"In today's world vandalism appears rampant."

6. Vandalism and Destruction of Property

A potentially expensive behavior problem which foster and adoptive families contend with is destruction of property at home or in the community. The behavior ranges from peeling wallpaper off walls to destroying hi-tech equipment at the local high school.

Destruction of property can be the result of the child's impulsive, thoughtless or unconsciously reckless behavior or the outgrowth of a hostile, deliberately planned, premeditated act. In the former case, impulse-ridden, hyperkinetic or explosively angry children may slam doors to the point where the hinges work loose. Or they might kick or punch holes in doors or walls during a hellacious temper tantrum. The destruction of property in these cases may be quite major and result in great expense (which is typically unreimbersable) to the family. During a rage one child, for instance, threw a hardball through the foster family's large screen TV. Home insurance did not cover this expense. An adoptive family had repeated episodes of plumbing problems due to their young adoptive son's fixation with flushing apples, toys and clothing down the toilet.

Premeditated destruction of property occurs both in the community and in home settings. In today's world vandalism appears rampant. With some acts of vandalism we cannot as a society fail to see, literally, the writing on the wall. Dead serious gang members as well as frivolous, gang member wannabees mark their turf with spray painted messages and secret codes. It does not take a nuclear physicist to read the anger between the lines. The increase in graffiti on walls, fences, signs and buildings seems ubiquitous these days.

"The child may lie when caught stealing, even when found
with 'the goods'."

7. Lying

Lying is one of the most frequently observed behavior problems in children who have been maltreated early in life. Lying can assume multiple forms. The child may lie when caught stealing, even when found with the goods. (One adoptive mother stated that her adopted son lied even when his hand was found literally in the cookie jar.) Or, the child may lie to build himself up in others' eyes, e.g. "I'm the fastest runner in school." Lying can be a manifestation of self-deceit, wherein the child denies the unpleasant or even painful realities of his life, past and present. In some instances, the child may have distorted reality to the point that he is convinced that his lies are truth.

Children who have been harshly treated early in life often do not trust adults enough to tell them the truth. They are afraid to admit to wrongdoings, failings and even truthful feelings, thoughts and opinions. In some instances these young-sters reflexively lie because an innocuous question from the adult is misperceived as an ominous interrogation. Thus, the child's feelings are held in check and opinions concealed. So thorough is his mistrust of the adult world, that his true self remains disguised, hidden or misrepresented.

In the most extreme instances, children who lie begin to derive a sick pleasure in "putting one over" on the world around them. Fooling others becomes comfortable, safe and eventually satisfying in itself. The child, through prevarication, controls what others know about him. His sneaky misbehavior as well as his most secret thoughts and feelings amount to living a lie.

"Stealing may be the most common problem seen in chronically maltreated children."

8. STEALING

Stealing may be the most common problem in chronically maltreated children. In fact, by the age of four or five, some children are accomplished thieves who pilfer tiny objects. By school age, stealing and hoarding of food (under beds, in closets, in secret caches), shoplifting from stores and even breaking-and-entering may occur.

The most typical underlying themes in children who steal are those of deprivation and entitlement. On the one hand, children who have been maltreated have felt deprived, cheated and unresponded to. That is, they feel that the world has not met their physical and/or emotional needs.

Some youngsters experience a sense of entitlement--a feeling that they have a right to take things they have been denied in the past. In kleptomaniacal children, the sense of entitlement is so pervasive that they will steal anything that is not locked away.

At times there may be nothing quite so empowering as feeling the victim. Children who have been the victim of neglect, deprivation and deeply unresponsive parenting often feel entitled (or perhaps empowered) to steal. As victims they feel justified in victimizing others with impunity. If another child has been given a gift for a birthday, for example, this may trigger a sense of having been slighted, overlooked or victimized. In response, the gift-less child may steal. A second case in point: if the foster or adoptive mother has spent time with another child, the ignored or victimized child may feel justified in stealing from the mother who is seen as neglecting him.

"Some foster and adopted children find a cloud of bad luck hangs over their unfortunate heads."

9. Low Self-Esteem and Depression

Children who have suffered months and even years of maltreatment frequently experience feelings of low self-esteem, dysphoria and depression. Many abused, neglected and exploited children have felt that their essential worth (or lack thereof) is indicated by the poor treatment they have received: "I was mistreated because I deserved it." "I was neglected because I was unworthy of parental attention." "I caused the sexual abuse I received." Abuse clearly has sent the child a message about his value.

Children who have experienced repeated parental rejection through threats of, or actual, abandonment also predictably develop a diminished sense of self-worth. That is, they mistakenly assume that they were undeserving of parental commitment. Similarly, children who drift from one placement (foster or adoptive) failure to another develop the notion that they are rejectable, worthless and unlovable. With histories of frequent loss and disappointment in important relationships, some foster and adopted children find a cloud of bad luck hangs over their unfortunate heads.

In some instances, foster and adoptive children experience a depth of dysphoric feelings which indicate full-blown clinical depression. These children may:

1) have poor appetites (or overeat);

2) sleep too much or too little;

3) be sluggish or easily fatigued;

4) have poor concentration and problems with indecision; and

5) show low self-esteem and a sense of hopelessness.

Lastly, frequent irritability and labile moods may indicate that the foster or adopted child is depressed. Psychiatric assessment may be helpful in diagnosing a depressive illness.

"A rolling child gathers no attachment."

10. Hyperkinesis

Webster defines hyperkinesis as "purposeless and uncontrollable muscle move ment". Foster and adoptive parents frequently report hyperkinesis in their children. Clinically speaking, hyperkinesis is often subsumed under the diagnosis of Attention Deficit Hyperactivity Disorder (e.g. A.D.H.D.). Hyperactivity, impulsivity and concentration problems are associated with that disorder. Children diagnosed with A.D.H.D. are frequently medicated with stimulant medication, e.g. Ritalin. However, hyperkinesis, and other symptoms mentioned above may not always indicate biologically or neurologically based A.D.H.D., but rather a form of psychological hyperkinesis related to early chaos in the foster or adoptive child's life prior to placement. Hyperactive behavior may also relate to an underlying depression. As such, hyperactive behavior may be a depressive equivalent. In many instances, children may act out their depression rather than expressing it in dysphoria, sadness, tearfulness, etc.

In foster and adoptive placements, hyperkinesis may play an undermining role in the formation of attachments. Indeed, the child that is constantly on the go, scattered and disorganized simply does not remain present with the parent figures enough to settle in, sink in and attach. As one child therapist aptly put it, "A rolling child gathers no attachments." Additionally, children who are consistently irascible with additional problems of impulsivity, hyperactivity and concentration difficulties may by their nature be difficult for others to grow close to.

"Poorly protected by others in the past, the child may feel most vulnerable in the dark..."

11. Insecurities and Fears

Many disturbed foster and adoptive children feel deep insecurities, anxieties and fears linked to early trauma and maltreatment. Some experience specific fears, while others hold onto a more general sense of unease and apprehension. Fear can be acute and paralyzing, as in panic states or phobias; or it may be less intense and yet gnawing and relentless, as in the child who chronically obsesses and worries.

In children who have been severely abused, physically or sexually, fears may be closely linked to triggering stimuli, e.g. to a bearded face reminiscent of the perpetrator; to the bathtub, because the child was abused in the tub; or, to their own bed, the site of past sexual abuse. Youngsters who have been repeatedly neglected, abandoned or otherwise rejected may show extreme fear of separation from significant others.

Nightmares, fears of the dark, fears of being kidnapped or harmed, and fears of separation from loved ones are common yet significant concerns of children who have been chronically maltreated. Especially at nighttime when the child is alone and without distractions, memories of abuse and abandonment may haunt him/her. Poorly protected by others in the past, the child often feels most vulnerable in the dark and may insist on sleeping with another youngster, with a pet or with his foster or adoptive parents.

"One foster father described the child as a 'cling-on', a child who wrapped his existence around another..."

12. Insatiable Neediness

Children with bottomless needs and unabating dependency often have experienced either: 1) chronic neglect of their needs, or 2) a symbiotic relationship to a parent who has overindulged the child but has also enslaved the child emotionally. In either case the child exhibits clingingness, unrelenting demands for attention from caregivers and the inability to entertain himself or function independently. One foster father described such a child as a "cling-on", a child who wrapped his existence around another in an emotional stranglehold.

When children show certain needy behaviors, one might easily mistake those as signs of the child's healthy attachment. However, though the child may clearly demonstrate attachment behaviors, underlying attachment actually may be highly overanxious and insecure, fleeting and fickle. The child might transfer willy-nilly his anxious attachment to another individual willing to endure his insatiable neediness. Many foster and adoptive parents, overtaxed by their child's incessant demands, grow painfully aware of how expendable they are to the needy child who seeks out any port in a storm.

"Many troubled foster and adoptive children...refuse to surrender the reins of control to adults..."

13. Oppositional Defiance and Stubbornness

Many troubled foster and adoptive children are "control freaks". Habitually oppositional, defiant and stubborn, they feel compelled to retain the upper hand, to refuse to surrender the reins of control to adults, and to obstinately reject any attempts to follow another's direction. Indeed, some children's answer to requests from the world around them is a resounding "NO!".

Oppositional or stubborn behavior may range from loud protestations and arguments to subtle noncompliance, e.g. "I forgot", "I didn't understand you", "I lost it", or "I didn't mean to". Ironically, children's defiant, stubborn behavior often necessitates increased attempts to control by caregivers. A bit conflicted, the child simultaneously resents and demands parental guidance. One perplexed group home parent asserted that if you let up with controls on Bobby, age eleven, that his obdurate, controlling behavior would worsen instantaneously. The counselor remarked wryly, "If you give this boy an inch, he thinks he's a ruler."

One of the more difficult parental challenges comes with the child who offers superficial, smiling agreement or promises to the parent's face, only to stubbornly fail to follow through with what was asked. Many foster and adoptive parents find themselves unable to determine if the child failed to understand what was said or simply refused to understand and comply. However, over time the pattern emerges of a child who retains control in the face of adult authority. Often these children have been previously raised in homes which were either tyrannical or chaotic. In the latter case, the child often took charge of his life by default. In the former, the child was allowed little or no reasonable, age-appropriate control or decision-making. In the face of such dictatorial control, the child learned insidious, surreptitious forms of rebellion.

Oppositional/defiant disorder is easily one of the most frequently seen diagnoses assigned to disturbed foster or adoptive children. The characteristics of this disorder are negativity, defiance, disobedience and hostility toward authority figures. While many children at various ages show these behaviors, the disorder is diagnosed when the pattern of rebellion and abstinence is pervasive and entrenched.

"One beleaguered adoptive mother described her son as 'the nitroglycerin child'. She never knew when he would detonate again."

14. Explosive Temper-Tantruming Behavior

Some disturbed foster and adoptive children are described as walking time-bombs. They have poor control of their tempers and "lose it", sometimes with an uncontainable explosion. They may, as small children, throw temper tantrums, hold their breath, bang their heads on the floor or bite themselves in rage. As older children and adolescents, they may break toys, kick holes in the walls or throw objects through the window pane. One beleaguered adoptive mother described her son as "the nitroglycerin child". She never knew when he would detonate again.

Parents who raise such explosively angry children find themselves constantly walking on eggs to circumvent blow-ups. These tiptoeing parents seem to never relax around the child with a Dr. Jekyl and Mr. Hyde personality. In some instances the parents never know when the next stormy personality change will occur.

What seems most difficult to ferret out for parents and professionals is how much voluntary control these children have over their anger. While some children use anger as a manipulative ploy to get what they want, with others the anger comes and goes in cycles not clearly linked to external events. In the latter case, there is an increased chance of an existing mood disorder, seizure disorder or intermittent explosive personality disorder.

"Love is a Trojan horse."

15. Paranoia/Mistrust

To children who have been abused, neglected, exploited and abandoned, love is a Trojan horse--a gift with dangerous surprises hidden within. Given their histories of disappointment and maltreatment, it is not surprising that some foster and adoptive children look askance at love. The outstretched hand of a loving adult is misperceived as an iron fist in a velvet glove.

The mental blueprint of the world to which the disturbed foster or adoptive child clings is distorted, twisted and cynical. Numerous negative encounters with maltreating individuals have rendered the child prematurely jaded. He expects the worst, especially in intimate relationships.

Paranoia and mistrust, along with many other behavior problems described in the previous pages, frequently emerge when the child feels a sense of burgeoning attachment to foster or adoptive parents. Severely disappointed by love in the past, disturbed foster and adopted children regard growing feelings of affection toward others with alarm. Paranoia and mistrust well up and acting-out behavior may emerge as the child's way of rejecting before he is rejected.

"Ironically, some children run away when they find themselves growing attached..."

16. Runaway Behavior

Children who run away from foster and adoptive homes are, in many ways, the most challenging to deal with. In fact, when they are on the run it is impossible to work with them, since, by definition, they are absent.

Children run for various reasons and to varying degrees. For instance, many children run to someone, e.g. birth relatives, boyfriend, etc. Other children run away from someone, e.g. a parent figure they perceive as unfair. Still other children run away when they find themselves growing attached, i.e. when intimacy begins to threaten a certain sense of safety in isolation.

One veteran foster mother observed, "Some kids are professional runners and others are recreational runners." The professional runners often disappear to big cities, live on the streets and never desire to return to adult caregivers, except for supplies or money. So-called recreational runners frequently have a different agenda; they typically run in order to have others chase after them. They run for the excitement of playing a dangerous version of "hide-and-seek".

"With some children, theatrical performances consume their every
action and interaction."

17. False Self/"As-If" Personality

Raised in an atmosphere of fear and oppression, many children learn to conceal true thoughts, feelings and opinions. They soon master the act of theatrics, drama and simulation of emotions. When the situation calls for disarming an adult, these youngsters can turn on the charm. Or, they let the tears fall, as needed. Insincerity, artificiality and shallowness mask underlying emotions of rage, depression and mistrust.

The child who has been chronically abused, neglected or sexually exploited may develop into an emotional chameleon, adapting a false self to each new human being he encounters. This child can adjust, perform and blend into many situations by feigning or manufacturing certain emotions, especially with adult caregivers. He may be quite adept at telling people what they want to hear. And, he can do it with increasingly persuasive drama.

With some children, theatrical performances consume their every action and interaction. To them life is a stage. A fully developed false self interacts with the outside world quite out of touch with the child's authentic feelings and hidden thoughts. Though he may appear childlike to the untrained observer, this child has become an "as-if" child--a caricature, acting "as-if" he were a normal, functioning child, but concealing his true identity behind the veil of a false self.

"Children who have been victims of early child abuse often act out with assaultive behaviors toward others."

18. Assaultive Behavior

Children who have been victims of early child abuse often act out with assaultive behavior toward others. These physical attacks can be directed toward adults or toward other children. Assaultive behavior includes the following: biting, kicking, hitting, throwing objects, pushing and tripping. The assaults may involve a weapon, a stick, a pipe or a closed fist.

Is it surprising that children who have chronically been maltreated by adults and who have encountered domestic violence would employ assaultive behavior toward others? These children often identify with the aggressor and act the part of a perpetrator of violence, rather than remaining in the role of victim.

Foster and adoptive parents, therapists and teachers who work with very troubled children sooner or later will be confronted with the child who is assaultive. The attack may come with or without a warning. The safety of both the child and others may be seriously compromised in these situations unless an adult is trained specifically to handle aggressive encounters.

"To emotionally promiscuous children people are like buses: in ten minutes
there will be another one coming along."

19. Emotional Promiscuity

One telltale sign of a young child's confusion about himself and others is emotional promiscuity, e.g. the strong tendency to approach and go off with almost anyone. Many younger children who have been chronically neglected, unsupervised and unloved indiscriminately reach out to adults they have just met. To these youngsters attachments to others are shallow, fleeting and quickly interchangeable. To emotionally promiscuous children people are like buses: in ten minutes there will be another one coming along. Love is cheap. Intimacy is replaced by what has been called, "instamacy", e.g. immediate skin-deep relating. So-called significant others are truly disposable and, in actuality, insignificant. Children who have been frequently rejected have few compunctions about discarding others at will.

Emotionally promiscuous children often display no stranger fear. In fact, they, as the saying goes, don't know a stranger. This emotional promiscuity frequently manifests itself when the child first enters the foster or adoptive home and immediately calls the parents, "Mom" and "Dad". Typically there is no sign of grief for others left behind--biological relatives or former foster parents. In the neighborhood these youngsters may quickly connect with the family down the street, while they distance themselves from their foster or adoptive family. In the psychotherapist or caseworker's office emotionally promiscuous children may hastily connect with the helping professional. Within moments of knowing the therapist or worker, for example, the young child may attempt to sit on his or her lap. In short order, the child may inquire about being adopted by the understandably startled professional.

A sad, but all too common, report from foster or adoptive parents is that, though their emotionally promiscuous child acts extremely dependent and clingy with them, he or she could be suddenly removed and placed with another family without even a backward glance.

"One adoptive father lamented, '...three months after we adopted I was taking an antidepressant and my wife was grinding her teeth and walking in her sleep.'"

CHAPTER THREE: Impact Upon the Foster or Adoptive Family

Very few parents know what to expect when they become foster or adoptive parents of disturbed children. They may have parented birth children successfully. Or they might have spent years teaching children in a classroom setting. Still other parents may have worked as mental health professionals providing psychotherapy to disturbed children. Though earlier experiences may help somewhat, they still leave the parents unprepared for life in the trenches of fostering or adopting the disturbed child. One adoptive father lamented, "We thought we were ready for parenting an emotionally disturbed child. However, three months after we adopted I was taking an antidepressant and my wife was grinding her teeth and walking in her sleep."

Chapter Three introduces the notion that the disturbed foster or adopted child can have a powerfully debilitating impact upon members of his new family. While traditional family systems theory holds that a disturbed family produces problem behaviors in its child, in foster care and adoption of special needs children the opposite may be true. That is, the disturbed child may produce disturbance in the foster or adoptive family dynamic.

"The child is the artist...and the painting."

1. The Effect of the Disturbed Child on the Family

It is well documented that children, as delightful and rewarding as they are, can have a debilitating impact on a marriage and family. The stresses and strains of parenting are well-known to most parents.

When a foster or adoptive child enters his/her new home, the impact can be highly stressful, especially when the child is emotionally troubled and the victim of past abuse, neglect or sexual exploitation. In effect, the foster or adoptive family imports the child's history into their family. Oftentimes such families, unsuspectingly fall victim to the child's historically distorted expectations about parents. In short order, the child evokes from these new parents negative feelings and behaviors which are as unfamiliar to, as they are unwanted by, the couple.

Due to the phenomenon of importing, the child often has a greater impact on the foster or adoptive family than they have upon him. Before you know it, the child has recreated an unhealthy parent-child relationship, which closely resembles pathological relationships he has experienced in the past. That is, the child exercises a potent influence upon his family. Rather than the passive recipient of parental influences, the child is an active player in influencing his new parent figures. Ultimately he has a hand in shaping family destiny in the foster or adoptive home. In this regard, it has been stated that "the child is the artist...and the painting".

"In short order, hapless foster or adoptive parents may discover that
the child is in charge."

2. Turning the Family Upside Down

In some foster and adoptive families, the disturbed child may wield more emotional clout than either parent. In a matter of days, significantly troubled children turn formerly confident parents on their ears with their misbehavior, power struggles, manipulations and divisive influence. In effect, the youngster refuses to surrender control to parent figures. He rejects the child role.

Many foster and adoptive children have experienced a great deal of neglect in their past. For that reason, they often found themselves without viable parent figures to take care of them. Beyond that, many of these children assumed parental roles toward younger (or older) siblings, and sometimes even toward their inadequate parents. As a result, once placed in a foster or adoptive family, they reject substitute parent figures who attempt to care for and discipline them. Furthermore, these children often attempt to assume the dominant role in the foster or adoptive family, sometimes with a great deal of success. In short order, hapless foster or adoptive parents may discover that the child is in charge.

"...in the 1950's a popular notion was that of the refrigerator mother as the driving force behind the child's noticeable psychopathology."

3. The Refrigerator Mother

There is a long-standing tradition of blaming mothers for their children's problems. Historically, discussion of the suspected cause of schizophrenia in children,
for example, centered on the mother. The so-called schizophrenogenic mother
was said to drive her child crazy by trapping him/her in no-win double-binds. It
was thought that the child perpetually received "damned if you do, damned if you
don't" messages from his mother. Unable to win his mother's acceptance, the
child checked out psychologically, becoming schizophrenic in the process.

The "blame Mom" craze spread to other areas of psychology and psychiatry. More
specifically, those who studied early infantile autism theorized that mothers of
autistic children were withdrawn, emotionally unavailable, psychologically icy, refrigerator mothers. I suspect that observations of mothers of preschool autistic
children, e.g. the age at which they were detected as nonverbal, atypical and withdrawn would have found women who were discouraged and removed from their
abnormal, unresponsive child. Though it is much more fashionable now to see
autistic children as born that way, in the past the refrigerator mother was viewed
as the driving force behind the child's psychopathology. More accurate is the
notion that the autistic infant had a profound effect upon the mother. Mothers
can be expected to appear quite removed and discouraged if they have given
birth to a child who is unusual, unreciprocal and non interactive from day one. In
such instances, the child refrigerates the mother.

The time-honored tradition of blaming mothers seems to be alive and well when
it comes to foster and adoptive mothers who are often fingered as the underlying
source of their children's significant disturbances. Incidentally, these mothers may
look "three French fries short of a Happy Meal", having attempted to raise disturbed foster and adoptive children. Thus, they might be easily mistaken as the
cause rather than the effect of the child's disturbance.

"In their efforts to control the out-of-control child, parents tend to try a number of approaches, most of which fail dismally..."

4. MOTHERS' EXHAUSTION

While some foster and adoptive mothers have experienced the negative effects of living with a withdrawn, unreceptive, icy child, others have endured the exhausting impact of raising scattered, driven and taxing children. Indeed, a growing number of foster and adoptive mothers (and fathers) are raising children who, due to special challenges of a neurological or neurochemical nature, bombard parents with unrelenting activity. These youngsters may be diagnosed with Fetal Alcohol Syndrome or Effects, with bi-polar (manic) disorders, or most commonly, with Attention Deficit Hyperactivity Disorder (A.D.H.D.). Children with A.D.H.D. are often impulsive, hyperactive and have attentional problems. Additionally, they are frequently disorganized, accelerated and require little sleep. Many have problems accepting limits and learning from consequences. As a result they often appear out-of-control. In their efforts to control the out-of-control child, adoptive and foster mothers attempt a number of approaches, most of which fail dismally or meet with only modest success. A summary of desperate parenting approaches described by Russell Barkley (1990) may be helpful.

1) Normal, typical parenting approaches are attempted. For example, the parents employ ignoring misbehavior. That is, they might actively overlook or withhold their attention from the naughty child. This approach is predicated on the assumption that the child's mis behavior serves to win negative attention.

2) When ignoring fails to make a dent in the misbehavior, the parents resort to frequent commands. The commands become more and more directive and repetitive, as the child does not seem to respond in any consistent or lasting way to the parent. Indeed, the child remains virtually as out-of-control after as before this approach is used.

3) As parental frustration mounts, parents issue threats to the child in their exasperated attempts to curtail misbehavior and to get the child to pay attention and to mind them. When threats seem to fall upon deaf ears, increasingly desperate parents switch to punishment, e.g. revoking privileges, isolating the child in his room, or spankings.

4) If all the above approaches prove futile and fruitless, parenting often decompensates by becoming less consistent and much more random in nature. Some parents are reduced to trying a shotgun approach, not sticking to any set game plan for curbing the child's behavior. Other parents, feeling sheer exhaustion and failure, cave into the child's continuing misbehavior. If, for instance, the child is failing to obey the parents' request to clean up his room, the parents may clean the room themselves. Or they will allow the child's assigned chores to go undone, rather than get into it with the child. Indeed, it may be less stressful to just do the chores themselves, or to let everything slide. Some parents find themselves waffling, alternating between overreaction to and withdrawal from the child.

Due to the fact that fathers and mothers parent quite differently and due to the child's tendency to react differently to each parent, marital difficulties frequently follow.

"Mothers, to whom the role of disciplinarian falls, are 'in the trenches with their kids'."

5. The Devolution of the Foster (or Adoptive) Mother

Sociological studies of working mothers indicate that these women continue to take on the lion's share of domestic chores (especially laundry) and parenting jobs. Even highly involved, dedicated males may fail to tackle an equal share of home and child-related duties. Though I have known many foster and adoptive fathers who are tremendous dads and pitch in around the house, there commonly remains a wide gender gap in parenting. This gap relates to both quantity and style of parenting. It certainly accounts for much maternal exhaustion and disillusionment and contributes to the devolution (not evolution) of the foster or adoptive mother.

Although there are undoubtedly many exceptions, fathers stereotypically adopt a playmate role in some families, staying less involved in the day-to-day discipline of the children and in the nitty-gritty details of their children's school and social lives. Mothers, to whom the role of disciplinarian falls, are on the firing line with their kids.

Most foster and adoptive mothers I have known rarely pass on the discipline to their husbands. The remark "Wait until your father gets home", commonly used by mothers of past generations, appears to be extinct. Assuming the disciplinarian role, mothers invite children's frustration and anger. The role of the "heavy" is for the most part a thankless job that falls upon the shoulders of mothers. It hastens the process of devolution.

Another factor affecting the downhill slide of foster and adoptive mothers, is that many foster and adoptive children have loved and lost previous mother figures. Deeply ambivalent toward female caregivers, they have reasons to desperately need as well as to distrust and resent mothers. For these reasons, foster and adoptive mothers often feel inordinate demands from their children; all the while these same children punish them for being mothers.

A foster father, dressed neatly in a two-piece suit and tie, asked me about his somewhat rumpled and exhausted better half, "Should I be concerned about my wife? She's begun wearing her hairdo a bit like Charles Manson." Given the imbalance in the household division of labor, given the disproportionate share of discipline provided by mothers, and given the extreme ambivalence disturbed children direct at them, is it any wonder that foster and adoptive mothers find themselves in a downward spiral?

"Fathers parent differently than mothers."

6. The Father's Role in All of This

Father's parent differently than mothers. There, I said it. Foster and adoptive mothers report with monotonous consistency that their husbands have a fantastic capacity to tune out the children's misbehavior, fights and cries, leaving them, the mothers, to deal with it. One bedraggled adoptive mother claimed, "The whole house could fall down around my husband as he reads the paper. Unless a piece of the ceiling plaster landed on his head, he wouldn't notice a thing."

Of course it is as unfair as it is oversimplified to assert that dad's are oblivious and uninvolved with their children. Many are exquisitely sensitive to children and intuitive in their parenting. However, the picture in many foster and adoptive homes is one of the father remaining a tad peripheral to the nuances of life with kids.

Unfortunately, this can be a setup for the divisive marital split which is promoted by many disturbed foster and adoptive children. Such youngsters may refuse to connect with, respect and obey their mothers, while paying homage to their father figures. In short, Mom is the "bad parent" and Dad, "the good". Under these circumstances fathers can be easily mislead by their wives' exasperation with the children. Experiencing these same children quite differently (e.g. "These kids seem normal to me.") from their wives, the dads erroneously assume that their spouses have lost it, perceive the child inaccurately, and have become overly disciplinarian and harsh. Many adoptive and foster fathers fail to see the seriousness of the child's disturbance, only recognizing that their wives have changed for the worse.

CHAPTER FOUR: Unconventional Strategies for Helping Children _____

D isturbed foster and adoptive children often fail to respond to conventional therapies and to orthodox parenting approaches. This has nothing to do with the general effectiveness or importance of those therapies and parenting approaches with other children. However, if and when foster and adoptive children fail to respond to the more traditional therapeutic and parental interventions, careful trials of more unconventional approaches might be in order.

THE OBJECTIVES OF UNCONVENTIONAL STRATEGIES

Although we will not articulate comprehensively the objectives of unconventional strategies here, the reader will find that elsewhere (Delaney, 1991; Delaney and Kunstal, 1993). Suffice it to say that the overall goals of treatment strategies should be to:

1) curb the child's acting-out behavior, e.g. behavior problems;

2) increase appropriate verbalization of feelings by the child;

3) improve the child's ability and willingness to negotiate with the adult caregivers; and

4) promote increased positive encounters with his foster or adoptive parents.

To protect both the foster or adoptive family and the child, strategies should be developed by the treatment team, which includes the child's therapist, caseworker, teacher, physician and (most importantly) the foster or adoptive parents and other family members. Strategies should be legal and within state regulations governing parenting. Additionally, they should be proactive, nonpunitive and strictly reflective of the child's age, emotional status, traumatic history, psychological needs, and physical health and well-being.

Chapter Four describes ten strategies which foster and adoptive parents have employed in situations where their child's current behavioral and emotional problems effectively thwart incorporation into the family. In such instances the family's attempts at reaching the child with affection and structure are stymied. Thus, the child successfully holds the family at bay and rejects the healing power of functional family life. When this occurs, the treatment team may need to devise intervention strategies which utilize one or both of the following general tactics:

1) paradox or reverse psychology; and/or

2) the unexpected, surprise and the infusion of new and different information to the child.

"Many of our interactions with disturbed foster and adoptive children are reduced to struggles over power."

A. Paradox and Psychological Jujitsu

Many of our interactions with disturbed foster and adoptive children are reduced to struggles over power, e.g. who will be in charge? The child, perceiving parents as unreliable, unpredictable and unresponsive, actively resists surrendering control to any parent figure, e.g. even the benevolent foster or adoptive parent. Further, the child obstinately refuses to re-learn new, more positive ways of interacting with other human beings. Or he clings fiercely to his obsolete notions about the adult caregivers around him. Indeed, it seems that the more we try to press the child actively to change, the greater the opposition and defiance we experience from him. He/she closes up, shuts down, moves away from us, and eludes change. The more we attempt to wrestle away inappropriate behavior and accompanying attitudes from the child, the more vigorously the child clings to historic patterns of thought and behavior. Soon, the entire parent-child relationship is mired down in power struggles--a pathetically unproductive wrestling match. Typically, a no-win situation develops.

When wrestling permeates the relationship, it may be time to consider other approaches which are less likely to evoke resistance from the child. "Psychological jujitsu", e.g. paradoxical approaches may be of assistance under these circumstances. Paradoxical approaches frequently involve prescribing to the child the very behavior in which he is engaged. These strategies avoid power struggles and psychological grappling with the child, while gradually using the child's negative and resistant energies to be neutralized and redirected along healthier pathways. For example, in place of forcefully wrenching misbehavior away from the child, we might paradoxically encourage the child to indulge in more of it, to the point at which the child insists that the behavior, his behavior, stops.

The five unconventional strategies discussed in this first part of chapter four will illustrate the use of paradox or psychological jujitsu. These strategies are:

1) Group Temper Tantrums;

2) Treating Head-Wait-Person Behavior;

3) Placing the Child in Charge;

4) The Art of Lazy Parenting; and

5) Putting High Technology to Work.

1. Group Temper Tantrams

The Brown foster family (with three biological, three adoptive, and two foster children) had tried all the conventional, good parenting approaches to the daily temper tantrums thrown by Billy, age 4. Among other things, they had carried him to his bedroom where he would not have an audience, but Billy tore up his room; they had rewarded him for rare episodes of peaceful acceptance of frustration of his needs; they had held him firmly and protectively in their arms to keep him from head-banging; and they had attempted to help him verbalize his needs and frustrations more effectively to reduce the acting-out. All conventional attempts to help Billy, however, appeared fruitless.

A "never say die" couple, Mr. and Mrs. Brown, after consulting with Billy's psychotherapist, decided to apply a more unorthodox strategy to interrupt Billy's temper displays in the home and community. They decided to join with Billy during his tantrums. More specifically, the next time Billy pitched a full-blown fit because he could not have sweets before supper, he threw himself onto the kitchen floor. Hearing the commotion, family members, as planned, converged on the small kitchen, knelt down on the floor to surprised looks from Billy, and then proceeded to lie down and roll around on the linoleum with him. Space was at a premium on the kitchen floor and the noise was deafening as the family threw themselves into the task enthusiastically. Mrs. Brown recounted later that with all the racket, she momentarily failed to notice that Billy had inched and wriggled his way out of the kitchen to the dining room where he sat staring in silent disbelief at the raucous display on the floor.

The Browns stated that this rather unconventional approach proved most effective in snuffing out Billy's temper tantrums at home. When complemented by their caseworker on their inventiveness, they revealed somewhat reluctantly, that they had also used the "group temper tantrum" approach in public!

A family which enjoyed doing activities together, the Browns even grocery shopped with all their children present. (To me, this would be flirting with disaster. But, to the Browns, it was, in their words, "No biggie".) In fact, they typically relished public outings, unless Billy erupted, which he did on one fateful grocery shopping day.

The shopping had gone without a hitch until the Browns, with a caravan of children in tow, started down Isle Four--the breakfast cereal isle. When informed that they would not buy sweetened cereal for him, Billy collapsed to the floor with a shriek. Without a word, family members looked first at Billy, and then at each other. In unison and almost as if on cue, the family members gathered around the child, dropped to their knees and then lay down and wriggled along side of Billy. (Billy must have thought that he was safe from group temper tantruming when he was in the public eye.) Billy stopped his misbehavior within a minute or so, but not before the family heard over the store intercom, "Tantrum on Isle Four!...Tantrum on Isle Four!"

2. Treating "Head-Wait-Person" Behavior

An experienced foster mother came into my office with an unusual story: "This past summer has been the worst of my life." She explained that her fifteen-year-old foster daughter, Michelle, was a giant syringe that sucked the blood out of the entire family. An extremely needy, dependent, "cling-on" adolescent, Michelle could not, in her foster mother's estimation, live without adult attention, even briefly. Nor could she cohabitate successfully with her peers for longer than a few moments. Within minutes of meeting young people her age, for example, Michelle would reveal to them that she had AIDS, which was untrue. Her false revelation, as you might expect, threw a monkey wrench into any possibility of friendship. Having burned her bridges at school with her peers, Michelle also wore out her welcome with teachers and other school personnel onto whom she would latch. Michelle set herself up for rejection in two key ways: one, she sabotaged friendships with her peers by making herself rejectable; and two, she exhausted adults with her insatiable demands for attention.

In the foster home Michelle's problems paralleled those in school. She set up the other children to reject her and exhausted the foster parents with constant need for adult attention. When asked by their therapist to give an example of how Michelle set up rejection from others, the perplexed and weary foster parents described Michelle's "Head-Wait-Person" behavior. They explained that Michelle attended to them at times as if she were a head waiter in a fancy restaurant. Specifically, when the foster parents sat down daily at the dining room table to converse for five minutes without interruptions from the children, Michelle suddenly, predictably appeared. She would then ask the foster parents, in fine head-wait-person form, "Could I get you something?" The foster parents asked the therapist, "How come we get so mad at her, when she is ostensibly being so nice?" The answer is, of course, Michelle's attentiveness to the foster parents is unwanted, unneeded, poorly timed and produces another demand upon them. Accordingly, the foster parents found themselves feeling increasingly impatient toward Michelle, and typically would remind her--the head-wait-person--to leave them alone. Michelle would walk away feeling hurt and reinforced in her belief that caregivers were ungrateful and she was unwanted. The foster parents felt somewhat guilty about sending the child away; thus, the encounter was lose-lose for both parents and teenager.

In listening to the foster parents, the therapist became convinced that an unconventional strategy with an element of psychological jujitsu might help. Here's what was tried. The foster parents agreed to use an approach which involved acting as if they were neurotic patrons in Michelle's ersatz restaurant. On the next occasion, e.g. the following day, Michelle interrupted the parents' private conversation in the dining room. The resultant interchange with her parents was certainly a surprise to Michelle.

Michelle: "Could I get you something from the kitchen?"

Foster mother: (pleasantly) "Thank you for asking, Michelle...as a matter of fact, you could go to the kitchen and pour us some coffee."

Michelle: (with a surprised look on her face) "You want coffee?...Sure, I'll be right back."

(Michelle then walks back to the kitchen and pours coffee into two cups and returns with them to the dining room.)

Michelle: "Can I get you something else?"

Foster father and mother: (after sipping the coffee) "Actually, Michelle, maybe you could add some sugar to the coffee. Could you please take the coffee back to the kitchen and add some sweetener, please?"

Michelle: (raising an eyebrow but forcing a smile) "Sure...no problem. I'll be right back."

(Five minutes elapse as Michelle sweetens the coffee, then returns to the dining room with the two cups of coffee.)

Foster parents: "Thank you very much, Michelle."

Michelle: (hoping she is finished) "Is everything okay now?...Or, can I get you something else?"

Foster parents: (in unison, after sipping coffee again) "We hate to be a bother, but what about some cream? Would you mind taking the cups back to the kitchen again?"

Michelle: (looking truly baffled but acting bravely) "I'll be happy to."

After this Michelle brought the sweetened, whitened coffee to her foster parents, but then they proceeded to change their minds, asking for black coffee. And then the sequence started over again. Finally, after twenty-five minutes of trips back and forth from kitchen to dining room, Michelle, setting the coffee cups down somewhat loudly, exclaimed, "What do you think this is, some kind of restaurant?!" Then she left the foster parents sitting alone at the dining room table.

Michelle's testiness at the end of this encounter was, for her, a temporary flight into healthier, more normalized adolescent relating. For what typical teenager waits on his or her parents hand-and-foot?

3. Placing the Child in Charge

Nine-year-old Corine was a control freak, according to the adoptive parents, and it was driving them crazy. Her control issues primarily focused on other children. Simply put, Corine had to be the boss. With other children she seemed to be hyper-alert to their misbehavior. She was always on duty, ready to tattle on any maleficence by the other children in the home. With the younger children there was always screaming when Corine was around, because she attempted to dictate how they dressed, when they ate and what they watched on television. She was parental toward them, but she was an overactive, harsh, tyrannical parent. With her older adopted brother, Robert, a fairly well-adjusted fourteen-year-old, Corine was unrelenting in one-upsmanship and in the pervasive struggle for who would get in the last word and who would be in charge. She attempted to tell Robert what to do and refused to take any direction from him when the adoptive parents left him in charge. All in all, the parents were perplexed with how to decrease Corine's obnoxious behavior. Constant reminders to her to mind her own business fell on deaf ears. The relentless vying for position of control among the children, usually spurred by Corine, was driving the parents up a wall.

In a world that has been frequently chaotic, tyrannical and unresponsive, children like Corine survive by attempting to take control in whatever way they can. For example, a child might attempt to control by refusing to do what he is told; or he might attempt to control intimacy by getting others to reject him; or the child might attempt to dominate or direct parent figures, friends or other children in the home.

Given the child's hunger for control, Corine's adoptive parents developed an unconventional strategy for intervening in this situation after many other approached had failed. It involved employing "psychological jujitsu", going with Corine's symptomatic behavior, rather than attempting to wrest it away from her. The parents placed Corine in charge of Robert and instructed him to request direction or permission from Corine in everything he wanted to do. After twenty-four hours of inane questions about what he should wear, what clothes matched with what, whether Corine would place a telephone call to a friend for him, and about what he could do to relieve boredom, Corine grew exasperated with the entire game.

She told Robert to make up his mind and struggle with his own decisions.

Of course, one installment of "Child in Charge" might not take care of all the extensive control issues that Corine has developed over early years of maltreatment. However, it pointed out a possible direction in which to head. Later, the adoptive parents used an approach of paying Corine to be in charge of Robert and of the younger children, as she previously had been exerting all that effort for free. The payment for that survival behavior helped Corine perceive her control somewhat differently. When she was not paid for controlling her siblings, she complained that she was working for "nothing". The complaint was a sign of moving toward healthier, more normal functioning.

4. The Art of Lazy Parenting

Sometimes we parents need to do less rather than more; decrease out efforts rather than increase them. Indeed, in many situations encountered with children who are emotionally disturbed and highly controlling to boot, "lazy parenting" might be just what the doctor ordered.

Case in point: Mr. and Mrs. White, a married couple with four adopted, school-age children (two boys and two girls), had grown increasingly exasperated with Beverly. An eleven-year-old fourth grader with average intelligence, Beverly was failing all her school subjects. The adoptive parents lamented, "Nothing seems to motivate her...she has no drive to achieve."

Despite parental efforts to help Beverly with her school work, grades remained low. Beverly consistently forgot to bring home her school work, books and assignments. Without this it was difficult for the adoptive parents to help her with work in the evenings. On the rare occasions when Beverly brought schoolwork home (after the parents threatened her), the child foot-dragged all night long, which prompted parental nagging. Furthermore, even if she had finished some homework, Beverly "lost" it on the way to school, and it was never turned in for credit. The parents felt they couldn't win, despite working overtime on Beverly's problem.

In situations like the above, parents often increase the amount of effort they put into making certain that homework gets done. They burn up calories in their futile attempt to light a fire under their unmotivated child. Sometimes the child may be dealing with a specific learning disability which has discouraged him/her over time. Specialized help at school may assist in that instance. On other occasions, the child may suffer from an Attention Deficit Hyperactivity Disorder which interferes with the ability to get school work organized. Medication along with psychotherapy may reduce impulsivity, concentration difficulties and hyperactivity to the point that school work becomes easier to start, stick to and complete. However, in some situations the child's difficulties with school have an emotional basis rooted in the child's need to control with passive resistance. Over time, the parents begin to work harder than their obstinate child. Checklists signed off by the school teachers sometimes help tighten the loop. (Often, however, the child "forgets" to get the checklist slip signed or "loses" the slip altogether.) Incentives and rewards may help if they are kept specific and short-term enough. Occasionally, grounding or removal of privileges may inspire the child to apply herself toward improved participation in school or completion of homework. Either professional tutoring or assistance by the parents may help, though the latter may become a battle-ground for parents and child.

When nothing seems to work, despite parental best efforts, then it may be neces-sary to employ "lazy parenting", as illustrated in the case of Beverly. Having tried consequences, rewards, reminders and everything else they could think of, the Whites were advised finally by their caseworker to do less, rather than more, to help Beverly.

"Maybe you're right in not wanting to work so hard in fourth grade," they told Beverly (without sarcasm). The adoptive parents took the paradoxical approach of giving Beverly permission to be held back a grade. They put her in total charge of remembering and completing her homework. Further, they stopped talking obsessively about it in the home. The Whites backed off and seemingly showed less interest in Beverly's academic life. In so doing, they attempted to remove themselves from a psychological tug-of-war with Beverly. One immediate result was that the adoptive parents paid much less negative attention to Beverly. In fact, they framed her behavior (or lack thereof) in a positive way, occasionally com-menting in a non-judgmental, matter-of-fact way: "Next year, if you are in fourth grade again, you will get to meet all sorts of new kids, e.g. this years third graders." Parental comments like these were interjected only periodically to provide Beverly information about the expected consequences of the decisions she was making on a daily basis. However, such reality checks were judiciously used and not over-done, for that would have invited possible argument from Beverly.

One other change that was made in the White home was the removal of the television, which was simply disconnected and stored. Beverly was not allowed to earn television time, nor was she told that TV was gone because of her poor school performance.

At first, Beverly's inertia remained unchanged (or perhaps worsened slightly), and Mr. and Mrs. White understandably feared that without any direction from them,

Beverly's chances of ever performing well in school were doomed. However, after three weeks, Beverly revealed confidentially to her therapist that she had begun to sneak homework into the house after school. Oddly, Beverly swore the therapist to secrecy, not wanting her parents to know that she had begun to do what they had been wanting all along! However, six months later, the secret was clearly out of the bag, when Beverly's report card came out with passing grades in all her subjects. The family was asked by the caseworker and therapist not to go overboard with praising Beverly, since that might trigger a regression.

5. Putting High Technology to Work

A foster mother came into my office looking quite haggard. "I have bags under the bags under my eyes," she complained wearily. Her newest foster child, an eight-year-old boy named Jamie, would not let her sleep. "He refuses to let me take an afternoon nap...he won't even let me get a good night's rest," she explained. "I have to get some rest soon, or I'll be worthless to him and to the rest of the family." The foster mother had a husband, an older birth daughter and two younger foster children, none of whom were getting any attention from her because of Jamie.

After a short discussion, the picture became clear. The foster boy was a highly anxious, worried, clingy boy who needed to physically hold onto the foster mother, or, at a minimum, keep her in sight at all times. If she walked into the back yard, he followed her. When she gardened, he followed so closely in her footsteps that once he was bumped on the forehead with the handle of the hoe. If she took a trip to the bathroom, he stood guard at the door. When she attempted to catch a few winks, he would silently steal into the room and stand next to her bed, staring into her sleeping face until her eyes popped open with a start. "He's going to give me a heart attack with this staring at me as I sleep," lamented this tired woman.

Especially when she tried to take an afternoon mental health nap, Jamie inevitably would interrupt her sleep. "I have even resorted to having my older daughter physically keep watch outside the bedroom door during my half-hour nap, but Jamie still has found ways to sneak into the room." (Once he had outfoxed the older girl by distracting her with a ruckus in another part of the house. Jamie then tiptoed into the bedroom when the girl went to check on things. On another occasion, Jamie climbed silently into the bedroom through the window.) The foster mother stated, "He is desperately persistent."

A review of this foster child's history revealed that he was a highly tense, insecure youngster who had experienced abject neglect early-on in his life. He had assumed a parental role with his birth mother who was alcoholic and substance-abusing. Jamie later informed his caseworker that many times he had found his mother passed out and totally unconscious when on a "bender". The boy would be understandably terror-stricken when he would fail to awaken her. He admitted that he had frequently feared that she was dead and would place a spoon under her nostrils to see if it fogged from her breath.

In addition to the fears of his mother dying from a deadly binge, Jamie also felt tremendous apprehension about abandonment by her. This fear seemed deeply rooted and was traced to the numerous occasions when his mother had disappeared without warning for long hours and even days at a time, leaving Jamie alone to fend for himself. Several times, she had left the child by himself for two weeks when she ran off with a total stranger, e.g. a truck driver she had met at a local tavern. As a kindergartner Jamie was found stealing candy at the local convenience store and was turned in to the authorities. Just before he was placed into the present foster home, Jamie had been found wandering a seedy downtown nightclub area at midnight. The boy was in a state of high anxiety, as his mother, in her drunkenness, had threatened to kill him if he didn't leave her to bar hop on her own. She then had turned and fled into the darkness of the downtown alleyways, leaving the young child terrified. In the foster home, agitated and wringing his hands as he agonized over his mother's whereabouts, Jamie was placed on a major tranquilizer to calm him to the point that he could sleep.

Given his history of neglect and abandonment, it was no wonder that Jamie was constantly shadowing the foster mother. His worries about her sleeping also made sense in light of his birth mother's episodes of "passing out". But the question remained, "How could Jamie be reassured to the point of allowing the foster mother her much needed, much deserved, rest?"

The inventive foster mother, working closely with the caseworker, devised a strategy involving the use of a Fisher-Price monitor--the type used in the nursery to allow anxious parents to listen in on their infants. In this case, Jamie was given the receiver which he clipped onto his clothing or held next to his ear. The monitor was placed on the night stand in the foster mother's bedroom. Jamie consequently could listen to the foster mother's every inhalation and exhalation. This approach seemed to very quickly soothe the child by offering him something very specific to do with his anxieties. He took his job of listening to the foster mother very seriously, especially during the first two weeks. However, as his anxieties lessened, he grew slipshod in his monitoring of her, to the point where the other children in the home would ask him, "How's Mom's nap going?" or "How does her breathing sound?" Eventually Jamie replied, "If you think you can do a better job of it, why don't you wear this dumb walkie-talkie?" Without struggling with Jamie to give up his symptomatic behavior, the foster mother had accomplished what she had intended all along: to help Jamie let go of his overanxious surveillance on his own time schedule. Psychological jujitsu to the rescue!

"Many troubled foster and adopted children require a hefty boost to lift them up the ladder toward more successful functioning."

B. The Use of Surprise, the Unexpected, & New and Different Learning

To help disturbed foster and adopted children we often need to assist them in experiencing new ways of relating to others and different ways of viewing themselves and others. Unfortunately, disturbed children become adept at evoking negative encounters with others which only allows a re-experiencing of the old way of life with its incumbent maltreatment, exploitation, lack of intimacy and failure to resolve conflict. Many troubled foster and adopted children require a hefty boost to lift them up the ladder toward more successful functioning. That boost often entails the use of unconventional strategies, employing the element of surprise, unexpected interactions and opportunities for new and different interpersonal learning.

While some unconventional strategies employ paradox or psychological jujitsu, others utilize the element of surprise, interjecting unexpected responses where hackneyed reactions were common, and introducing the child to fundamentally new and different ways of expressing himself within the family. "Surprise, the unexpected and new and different learning" can dislodge children's old perceptions and rigid behavior patterns.

In this last half of chapter four, five unconventional strategies, which employ the element of surprise, the unexpected and the experiencing of the new and different will be discussed. They are:

1) The True Meaning of Christmas...Or, Hannukah;

2) Planned Ignoring of Misbehavior;

3) Running Away from the Runaway Child;

4) Screaming Your Heart Out; and

5) Bellowing From the Basement.

1. The True Meaning of Christmas...or Hanukkah

An adoptive family with a sibling group of three foster/adoptive girls, seven, nine and eleven, had witnessed gradual progress in the three sisters over the eight months following placement. Firesetting had disappeared, stealing was on the wane and nightmares had subsided. However, with the onset of the Christmas season, they noticed a sharp regression. The youngest girl inexplicably set fire to the carpeting in her bedroom on half dozen occasions. The middle daughter began masturbating almost constantly and had nightmares every night. The oldest began running away from home. These and other problems, once thought to be solved, began to reemerge in spades. What had triggered them? What was bothering the girls?

In psychotherapy the three sisters gradually revealed what was at the core of the behavioral eruption. These three foster/adoptive girls were terrified by the approach of the holiday season. What came out in their recounting of the past was a history of ritualistic, satanic, sexual abuse. The biological parents practiced demon-worship with witchcraft thrown in for good measure. During Christmas season these disturbed parents decorated a dead fir tree with black crepe paper and sexually perverse and devilish ornaments. The culmination on Christmas day entailed the parents presenting the children with pornographic sex toys, explicit, X-rated movies and other twisted holiday gifts. Then the parents proceeded to sexually abuse the three girls, which abuse they videotaped for distribution to fellow satan worshippers and cult members. For cooperating, the girls were given piles of more presents before the day's end. Gifts for sex.

With this horrible and painful disclosure, the therapist and adoptive parents then knew why the Christmas season had precipitated such sharp increase in behavior and emotional problems.

Given what their daughters had been through in past Christmas seasons, the foster/adoptive parents decided to restructure the Yuletide experience. In fact, they voluntarily suggested to the therapist that they become Jewish during December. Their thinking was that the girl's memories of Christmas past were so horrific that celebrating something completely different might be the only way to transcend those historic hurts. The therapist thought that the foster/adoptive parents suggestion was very charitable and sensitive to the girl's remaining issues about sexual abuse at Christmas time. However, the therapist recommended that the family de-emphasize the materialism of Christmas (e.g. which conjured up gifts-for-sex memories for the girls) and emphasize the spiritual aspect of those holy days. In the end, the strategy was to use the Christmas experience to educate the girls about family values, giving love to others in the family and about the religious significance of Christmas.

2. Planned Ignoring of Misbehavior

Ignoring children's misbehavior can be a helpful strategy in dealing with some behavior problems in foster and adoptive children. Now, it goes without saying that we cannot ignore certain behaviors, such as fire-setting, sexual acting-out, and assaultive behavior toward others. However, some outlandish behavior can be dealt with more effectively by, in effect, doing nothing--except to make oneself scarce.

Case in point: One Thursday I showed up for my weekly consultation meeting with group home parents at a local residence in my home town. Walking in after ringing the door bell, I found a small crowd of boys surrounding the prostrate and writhing body of one of their house mates. This unfortunate boy had been bounding down the stairs from the second floor, taking three steps at a leap--until he missed, and in the process he sprained his ankle.

As we comforted him, another child came in from the backyard, announcing in excitement, "Bobby is going to jump! Bobby has climbed to the top of the tree! He's going to jump!" Immediately, in response to this news, the small crowd dispersed and hustled to the back yard. Quickly, the curiosity-seekers (myself included) surrounded the base of a large cottonwood tree which swayed in a stiff breeze. Bobby, clinging to the flimsy branches near the top of the tree, was screaming that he was going to jump. (I should explain here that Bobby is the penultimate "99% child", by which I mean the sort of young man who routinely demands 99% of the attention from adults and sometimes from children too, leaving the 1% to be equally distributed among the rest of the family members. When the other boy had sprained his ankle, Bobby had suddenly needed to devise some way of winning back center stage.)

Fortunately, as a psychologist I had taken coursework in crisis management, and so was comfortable in yelling comforting, empathic words up the tree toward Bobby. Unfortunately, my kind remarks had little persuasive impact on him. To my chagrin, the crowd of boys around the tree tried a different, less compassionate approach. "Jump, Bobby, jump!" they began to chant in unison. "Jump, Bobby, jump! Jump, Bobby, jump!" they taunted him.

The group home father appeared in the nick of time and spoke out forcefully to the crowd, "Okay, I want everybody back in the house. Right now!" "That's right, guys. Better do exactly what he says," I reinforced. "You, too, Dr. Delaney," shot back the group home parent. Nodding with sudden insight, I shuffled back, chastened, into the house. Until that moment I had not seen that I, along with the crowd of unsympathetic boys, had become part of the problem.

Back inside the house, we attended to the sprained ankle. After no more than five minutes, Bobby, miffed and a bit scuffed up from scaling down the tree, stalked in through the back door, wondering where his audience had gone.

(Note: It is important to reiterate at this point that dealing with children who are engaged in suicidal or self-destructive acts, or, who are threatening to do so, should not be taken lightly. In the case described above, the group home parent had extensive knowledge about Bobby and how Bobby had reacted in the past. That is, the group home parent was not capriciously and dangerously calling Bobby's bluff.)

3. Running Away from the Runaway Child

Jerry, age twelve, was a recreational "runner" who thought it good sport to disappear each night after supper time. Upon finishing his dinner, Jerry would immediately jump up from the table and saunter out the door. "It's your night to do the dishes, Jerry," his adoptive mother would yell after him. "You've got homework," added his adoptive father. "It's dangerous to be out in the dark in this neighborhood," reminded the three younger children in the home.

All of the comments from family members were of no importance to Jerry, who bolted from the house with a smug "you can't tell me what to do" sneer on his face. He then disappeared under the cover of darkness as his adoptive father pursued him out the door. Jerry was swift of foot, and his father could never catch up with him or successfully track him down.

Jerry's adoptive parents were quite concerned about the nightly disappearances, as Jerry would sometimes be gone for two hours or longer, only later sneaking back into the house. Each morning Jerry appeared at the breakfast table as if nothing had happened. He refused to talk about it and went off to school without a word. The adoptive parents resorted to phoning the police, who had as little luck in locating Jerry as the parents had. Indeed, after a few weeks of cat-and-mouse with Jerry, the police adopted a "don't call us, we'll call you" attitude with the family, referring them to social services. Soon, the adoptive parents were relegated to the role of searching for Jerry. Scouring the neighborhood on foot, calling the homes of Jerry's friends, and patrolling the streets outside the immediate neighborhood were all equally unproductive in finding the boy. Then, Jerry would reappear miraculously, unmolested and unmoved, and go to his room in arrogant silence. What could the family do? The adoptive parents did not want to lock Jerry in his room or physically restrain him. Grounding, pleading, promised rewards for compliance, and threats of removal of privileges fell upon deaf ears. Jerry was successfully playing "hide and seek", and no one could stop him. What's more, the adoptive parents felt themselves hostages in their own home.

Dutifully, they kept their nightly vigil for the prodigal Jerry. Rarely, if ever, did the parents go out on a "date" as a couple. Seldom did they take the other children to a movie as an entire family. Ever concerned about Jerry's whereabouts, they hunkered down for their nightly worry session, with Jerry "on the run".

After several weeks of this, Jerry's adoptive parents received an interesting telephone call from a nosy neighbor lady down the block from them. This woman called with a question: "Why does your son hide under my porch every night in the dark with binoculars?"

The adoptive parents quickly surmised that Jerry had been playing a game of cat-and-mouse with them and having a good laugh at the family's expense. They talked with their family therapist about a new strategy for dealing with Jerry's runaway behavior, now knowing about the prank he had been playing on them.

The next evening, Jerry jumped up from his dinner plate and bolted for the door. In unison, the parents yelled after him, "Sorry you couldn't join us, Jerry!" Jerry's head swiveled around with a curious look as he continued out the door into the night. That night, no one pursued him into the darkness. Back at home, the family quickly mobilized, jumping into the family mini-van, then backing out of the garage and slowly navigating down the street in the direction of Jerry's hiding place. With the windows rolled down, the family sang loudly and playfully, "Let's all go to the Dairy Queen..." (Jerry's favorite food in the entire universe was ice cream.).

Of course, the family had not merely abandoned Jerry to his own devices, since they were concerned about what he might do alone in the neighborhood. By agreement with the "nosy neighbor lady", the adoptive parents had arranged for her to watch Jerry closely and to be in touch with them on their cellular phone if there was a true emergency to deal with. However, the neighbor reported later that Jerry scrambled from under the porch and stared after the retreating mini-van with the ice cream lovers inside. He then sauntered down the block to the family home, where he discovered the doors locked. Jerry stood impatiently on the front steps under the outside light, periodically checking his watch as he waited to rejoin his family.

(Note: The strategy employed above would not be advisable with all runners and should be discussed in detail with the therapist and caseworker who know the child. As with any of the strategies described in this book, certain tailoring of the approach would need to reflect the child's individual needs, issues and his potential for self-harm. However, in the case described above, it was just what the doctor ordered. Jerry quickly dropped the running behavior in favor of joining the family on what soon became a nightly tradition, e.g. the trip to the Dairy Queen.)

4. Screaming Your Heart Out

A seasoned foster mother once confided in me wistfully, "My one prayer in life is that I lose my hearing." I immediately laughed, but she set me straight. "I'm not kidding. I am so frustrated with Timmy and his screaming, conniption fits." (Timmy was a four-year-old with probable fetal alcohol effects and the lungs of Luciano Pavorati. Among other things, Timmy frequently let loose with ear-piercing screams that, in the foster mother's words, could "awaken the dead".)

What can a foster or adoptive parent do with the child who emits such painful cacophony? Some screaming children literally go on for hours, while parental nerves stand on end. Other children grow restless and join in the chorus, as if the screeching were contagious.

Parents often report that therapists, caseworkers and other helping professionals recommend that they count to ten in these situations. (One foster mother retorted, "Make that ten thousand!") Another suggestion from professionals is to place the child out of earshot, if possible. (One adoptive father stated, "When I put him in the garden level of our house, he defecated on the carpet and smeared it into the nap.") Still another word of professional advice is to be impeccably consistent and firm so that the child eventually drops the behavior as unproductive (However, one exasperated adoptive mother lamented, "We've been consistent with our adopted daughter for three months...When will the screaming end?")

Returning to the case of the mother with the "deaf wish", Timmy, her foster son, screamed every time she put him in the car for their hour-long ride to the physical therapist's office. Initially, he screamed the entire way. Pulling off the highway for a brief time-out did not have the desired effect. Talking in subdued or firm tones produced nothing. What was the foster mother to do?

Working closely with her caseworker and the child's psychotherapist, the foster mother ultimately arrived at two strategies which curbed screaming. At home, she used tape--not duct tape!--audio and video taping Timmy during his scream-fest. While videotaping Timmy for the psychotherapist (e.g. so he could experience what the fits were like at home), she discovered that he clammed up whenever he saw the camera or tape recorder. Timmy also refused to view videotapes of his tantrums after the fact.

Given Timmy's propensity to fall silent when taped, another approach was tried using a similar form of feedback. Specifically, a "talking parrot doll" was employed during the car rides. (Any novelty shop carries this stuffed animal which uses a noise-activated process to almost instantly echo back whatever sounds it picks up.) This echolalic parrot, placed on the dashboard, was used with Timmy when the mother was driving. Luckily, Timmy, sitting in the back seat, could not tolerate the obnoxious sound of his own screams coming back to him over and over again from the parrot's beak. He then would quiet down in the car.

5. Bellowing from the Basement

Jennifer, age seven, had been adopted at the age of four. Initially, she showed no fear of strangers. To the contrary, she would walk off with almost any stranger while remaining avoidant of her adoptive parents. The adoptive parents described Jennifer as a "user friendly" child--one who was friendly to those who would use or exploit her.

Other problems became quite evident shortly after her adoption. Jennifer would not ask for food at the table, but preferred to steal food in midnight raids. She lied reflexively and smiled to cover angry feelings. All in all, these problems did not make Jennifer an easy child to love. The adoptive parents perceived her as fake and artificial, rarely ever showing honest feelings to them. People who valued truthfulness and candor, these parents were regularly put off by Jennifer's artifice. Her "don't get mad, get even" approach led to odd, irritating behaviors that further aggravated the adoptive parents. If mad, Jennifer sat stone-faced or grinning inappropriately, while she secretly plotted revenge.

Missing in her behavioral repertoire were typical, expected childhood actions and verbalizations addressing the meeting of her needs. That is, she never complained, pleaded with her parents, persuaded, cajoled, argued with them, whined, pestered, and/or otherwise vented feelings or expressions of her needs directly. Seemingly unable to stand up for her rights, she remained a perpetual victim. This sense of victimization appeared to keep her passive and to spur her to act vindictively and secretly. The adoptive father remarked about this: "For Jennifer, there is nothing as empowering as being a victim. It helps her to justify her sneaky misbehavior."

Ironically, as passive as Jennifer acted around her parents, she was quite aggressive toward children and things. For example, she pushed two children down the steps intentionally. When sent to her room, she would peel wallpaper off the walls or urinate down the heat duct. While in time-out in her room, which was in the lower level of the house, Jennifer never appealed to her parents to allow her to come out. "She would stay there forever...she is so stubborn that she refuses to ask to come out, as if it didn't matter to her...which it really does," asserted her adoptive father. Instead of calling out for her parents to let her out of time-out,

Jennifer would work through emissaries, the other children. She would convince the younger children to argue her case before the adoptive parents.

The strategy which the adoptive parents employed here was to insist that Jennifer become more assertive, overtly demanding and forcefully articulate her needs. They tried several approaches, but one in particular stands out from the rest: namely "Bellowing". Specifically, the parents encouraged--no, demanded--that Jennifer speak up for herself when she had been placed in her room for a time-out (which occurred a few times each week). When Jennifer felt ready to come out of her room--typically after ten minutes or so--she had to say so audibly. Since Jennifer's room was located in the basement, she had to literally bellow to be heard. Her adoptive parents sometimes would yell back to her that they could not hear her clearly, though they really could. This irritated Jennifer, who would then scream all the louder that she was ready to come out!

After two or three weeks of the "bellowing" strategy, the adoptive parents reported that, if they hadn't know better, they would have thought that Jennifer was getting worse. She had begun to slam doors, scream out her anger and stomp through the house when she was mad at them. Interestingly, now Jennifer was doing "her job", i.e. she was vocalizing her anger, rather than eliciting it from others. During one temper display, Jennifer, yelled at her father, "I liked it better when I was in charge!" She sobbed loudly and finally, exhausted, was held by her father who assured her, "It's okay to be mad, but *we* have to be in charge. When you are grown-up, *you* can be in charge."

Both adoptive parents have remarked that Jennifer has begun to soften to the touch and has become more real in her embraces. They feel quite delighted that she has begun to show much more authentic, genuine feelings in front of them. This open display of emotion has permitted, according to the parents, "a million discussions" with Jennifer.

CHAPTER FIVE: Discussion of Special Issues

Chapter Five addresses four issues which merit special discussion:

1) idealization of the birth parent with corresponding devaluation of the foster or adoptive parents;

2) the child's search for birth family;

3) classic triggers which precipitate strong responses in children who have experienced chronic separations and losses; and

4) resiliency in children.

Before turning to graphic depictions and commentaries on these issues, it may be helpful to put them in context.

First, idealization/devaluation is often a very painful issue for foster and adoptive parents to experience. For all their devotion to the child, these parents often find that they receive little gratitude from, or even acceptance by, the youngster. While most foster and adoptive parents are not in it for the gratitude or acceptance, they do--and not unreasonably--expect something other than total thanklessness and rejection from their charges. It is extremely difficult for foster and adoptive parents to reconcile the fact that they are doing much, if not all, the hard work with a child, while the child demeans them. In addition, it is particularly discouraging for foster or adoptive parents to observe the child extolling the virtues of parent figures who have grossly mistreated them in the past.

Secondly, the issue of the child's search for roots is a predictable and normal part of growing up as a foster or adopted youth. The search predominantly relates to identity formation, but unfortunately on occasion it can become a battleground within the foster or adoptive home.

Thirdly, when children have experienced unsettling disruptions, dislocations and losses in their early lives, they are sensitized to changes within and around them. Occurrences which might seem commonplace to others may stimulate overwhelming feelings of loss, abandonment and anxiety in youngsters who are loss-sensitive. It may help to have foreknowledge about what issues trigger vulnerable foster and adoptive children's fears of separation and loss.

Lastly, though recent studies indicate that some children fare better than others under traumatic circumstances, the belief that youngsters are endlessly resilient is misguided.

"The child, in effect, places his birth parent on top of a pedestal, while burying his current parent figures under the pedestal."

1. Idealization/Devaluation

Foster and adoptive mothers and fathers often face an issue which impairs the relationship between themselves and their new offspring. The issue is idealization of the birth mother (or other previous parent figures) along with corresponding devaluation of the current foster or adoptive mother or father. In the process of idealization and devaluation, the child, in effect, places his birth parent on top of a pedestal, while burying his current parent figures under the pedestal.

Idealization/devaluation often effectively stymies the promotion of a warm, balanced, realistic relationship with the foster or adoptive parents. Foster or adopted children may canonize their birth parents as saints, even if these parents have been flagrantly abusive or neglectful. At the same time, these children may scapegoat the foster or adoptive parents, comparing them unfavorably with their other parents. Splitting (as described earlier between foster or adoptive mother and father) may occur between foster/adoptive and birth parents: foster/adoptive means "bad" parent, birth means "good" parent.

The child's idealization of the birth parent or his/her cherished memory of the biological family may not necessarily indicate a healthy attachment. Indeed, many of the most insecurely attached and sorely neglected children will maintain an idealized picture of parents who may have mistreated them horribly. In some instances, the child remains unconscious about deep feelings of disappointment, rage and hurt which attach to his biological parents and their chronic failures in nurturing him/her. For various reasons the child has denied, repressed, split-off or deliberately suppressed the negative feelings toward those figures. Consequently, those strong emotions are displaced onto the safe, undeserving targets of the foster or adoptive parents.

"The child's desire to understand, reconnect with, and come to grips with the past is not a sign of failings of the foster or adoptive parents."

2. The Search for Birth Family

Closely related to the issue of idealization/devaluation is that of the child's search for birth family. Some research has shown, for instance, that a large percentage of children placed in long-term, permanent foster care ultimately return to live, at least for a time, with biological family members. Similarly, adoptive parents frequently observe that their adopted children express the desire to search, e.g. to trace their roots, to connect somehow with their blood ties.

The child's desire to understand, connect with, and come to grips with the past is not a sign of failings of the foster or adoptive parents. To the contrary, if the child can vocalize this normal interest it may be evidence of the trust he feels and the openness that exists within his foster or adoptive home.

To reduce the chances that the search issue becomes a battleground or an underground struggle, it is best for adoptive and foster families to deal with the feelings openly and proactively. While an actual reunion with family members may not be advisable in some instances, in other cases the youngster may require some sort of direct contact to satisfy curiosity and perhaps to resolve crucial underlying feelings about personal or ethnic identity. Whatever the case might be, the foster or adoptive family (sometimes with the help of the caseworker or therapist) should help their child identify what his/her urge to search means and cooperate with the child in a forthright and realistic fashion to address the issue.

"Some children are so loss-sensitive that even a seemingly harmless visit with their caseworker may trigger fears of being moved again."

3. Triggers to Loss-Sensitive Children

Disturbed foster and adoptive children often have had histories rife with chronic separations from, and losses of, significant attachment figures. In many instances they are emotional nomads, moved from pillar to post--sometimes with no warning, no explanation and no plan. Foster care drift can become the rule with children who remain in the system for more than a few months.

Given their early history of loss and instability, it is characteristic of these nomadic, insecurely attached children that certain key incidents will trigger strong feelings, regression and acting out behavior. The following list enumerates some of the classic triggers which evoke strong responses in loss-sensitive children:

1) A new child is moved into the placement.
2) The birth of a child in the placement.
3) Illness in the foster/adoptive parent.
4) Respite weekend or vacation by foster or adoptive parents.
5) The beginnings of feeling love/trust for the family.
6) Finalization of adoption.
7) Cancelled or shortened visits by biological parents.
8) Approaching court dates.
9) Developmental stirrings of adolescence.
10) A child is moved out of placement.
11) Anniversary reactions.

Many of the behavioral problems mentioned earlier can be triggered by one or several of the incidents listed above. Some children are so exquisitely loss-sensitive that even a seemingly harmless visit by their caseworker may trigger fears of being moved.

"The phoenix with the human smile..."

4. Invulnerability & Resiliency in Maltreated Children

During a foster parent support group meeting, a "new recruit" couple talked about their feelings of discouragement and hopelessness in dealing with two severely abused foster children--their first! Turning to veteran foster parents in the group, they asked, "How do you do it? How do you hang in there with these kids? Knowing what they have been through, how do you keep your optimism? Can we ever really help them? Do they eventually recover? Will they ever bounce back?"

Over the past three decades, researchers have studied the effects of child abuse, neglect and sexual exploitation on children (and on adult survivors). They are searching for resilient, invulnerable kids--those who transcended their early traumas, who went on to lead successful lives, and who bounced back.

But is any child truly unaffected by maltreatment? Are maltreated children the psychological equivalents of steel-belted radial tires that seal over punctures and survive all manifestation of hazards on life's highway?

THE INVULNERABILITY MYTH

In the words of Lois Murphy and Alice Moriarity, "There is no completely invulnerable child." In fact, infants who are initially, inherently robust will ultimately succumb to multiple or cumulative stresses and traumas which beset them. In a word, there is a limit, a definite limit to any child's capacity to cope with, adapt to, and overcome the vagaries of an unkind world. Ultimately, without escape, relief and protection from harm, the child decompensates. So what of the so-called invulnerable, super child? Is talk of such hardiness wishful thinking? Is it naive to cling to the fantastical hope that significantly maltreated children can endlessly rise from the ashes of misfortune, the phoenix with a human smile?

Total and thorough invulnerability is a myth, pure and simple. Serious abuse, neglect and/or sexual exploitation almost inevitably leave emotional scars and psychological vulnerabilities. For that reason, it may be more realistic to direct research toward partial invulnerabilities and toward factors in the child or his/her

"There is a breaking point for each child--a point at which the capacity
to bend and stretch stops and some breakage occurs."

environment that soften the effects of maltreatment and trauma. Further, focus should be placed upon the specific reparative interventions which build on the child's vestiges of invulnerability and which exploit in a positive fashion the child's acquired survival behaviors. Survival behaviors, which are often described in more negative terms as symptoms, may hold the seeds for healthy growth in the child. Interventions and strategies which can beat swords into plowshares may transform distorted, negative behaviors of the child into healthier, positive ones.

Returning to the question of the invulnerability myth, I hesitate to apply the term "invulnerable" or "invincible" to abused or otherwise maltreated children, since there is a breaking point for each child--a point at which the capacity to bend and stretch stops and some breakage occurs. At that juncture, psychological damage becomes virtually inescapable. There is some fundamental emotional toll taken upon the child.

There is a second reason for hesitating to use the term "invulnerability", for it may offer a false impression that children's recuperative powers are so strong that we need not worry about to what they are exposed. The reality is that, afloat in an ocean of uncaring, no child is truly unsinkable. Indeed, invulnerability--unsinkability--may be used as an argument for leaving children too long in untenable, unlivable and untreatable home lives. Similarly, it may provide bogus justification for capriciously uprooting the child from a loving foster or adoptive home without concern for the emotional cost to the child.

Case in point: Baby Jessica DeBoer. Following her move from her "psychological parents", who had adopted her, to the alien household of her birth father and mother, the press corps interviewed an expert on adoption, who was quoted (I am paraphrasing), "Children are resilient and adaptable". In the abstract, it may be true that children are hardy and plastic; however, their malleability is neither boundless nor without a price. Is there anyone, parent or professional, who would assert that Jessica would not have experienced the unconscionable "death" of her psychological parents by her uprooting from home and hearth? Is there anyone who could claim that her unfortunate emotional dislocation would not eventually impact all future love relationships in incalculably negative ways? In this regard, Ellen Farber and Byron Egeland warn, "There is an ethical issue to consider when spreading the notion that there are children who are invulnerable to abuse...Social scientists have to be responsible in discussing invulnerability, lest policy makers come to

"We do not believe that many children can develop coping skills and be emotionally healthy in a chronically abusive or neglectful environment."

harbor the idea that if children are only strong enough, they will survive. We do not believe that many children can develop coping skills and be emotionally healthy in a chronically abusive or neglectful environment."

HARD DATA ON INVULNERABILITY AND RESILIENCE

Research in the area of invulnerability remains in its infant state. However, it does appear that certain children do hold up remarkably well under stressful circumstances of poverty, tragedy and loss. Indeed, some of these children appeared to rebound vigorously following the strain of significant disruption in their young lives. These children, dubbed "good copers" by Murphy and Moriarty, recovered from serious misfortune by means of:

1) sequestering themselves in a safe place;

2) removing themselves for a time to heal;

3) utilizing self-soothing activities; and

4) employing symbolic play and fantasy to either act out traumatic themes or to escape, if only briefly, harsh realities.

Data about recovery, resiliency, invulnerability, etc. suggest that children who had been abused very early in life rebound to a level of competence by the age of four or earlier, if they experience a dramatic improvement in life style, e.g. improved home stability, placement in foster care, or entry into quality day care settings. However, it should be noted that none of the children who rebounded had come from severe maltreatment. Farber and Egeland cautioned, "Children with a history of chronic and severe maltreatment were observed to have serious behavior and adjustment problems by the time they reached preschool age. We did not find any invulnerable children among this group. Even though some of the moderately maltreated children were competent, we are pessimistic about their future."

INVULNERABILITY IN THE TRENCHES

Those of us entrusted with the lives of abused, neglected, exploited children, of course, rarely observe the child who has emerged from the abyss of abuse totally unscathed. Residential treatment centers, foster and group homes and special needs adoptive families encounter daily those children who are, psychologically speaking, "the walking wounded". Those who live with, love and otherwise assist these vulnerable children, understand the limits to the child's capacity to endure injury. Although we feel admiration for and astonishment at how these youngsters have survived their appalling past, we seldom believe that they have transcended trauma without damage. A delicate bubble has burst; childhood dreams have turned nightmarish; and an innocence has died.

Yet we look for signs of life within. Recently, after the tragic terrorist bombing of the federal building in Oklahoma City, sleep-deprived workers struggled around the clock searching with dogs, sound equipment and cameras, peering into the rubble, ears cocked, gently probing for pockets of life. This is a metaphor for those of us who work with children whose early lives were demolished. If we can uncover the "pockets of life" within each troubled child in placement, we are provided with an opening. These pockets are the remains of resiliency, the traces of invulnerability upon which we can build, or rebuild, young lives.

To reiterate, none of those children in residential care, foster, group and special needs adoptive homes have escaped the past unscathed. These youngsters come into the world of new caregivers with old world views, cynical expectations and patterns of negative, abnormal behaviors which are mystifyingly out of place in their new, protected environment. These survival behaviors are the vestiges of harsher times. Although these behaviors are problematic and obsolete, ironically they may provide opportunities for a healthier level of survival and change.

Therapeutic interventions with children in care should strive to decipher the meaning of the child's survival behaviors and should redirect the psychological energy employed in maintaining dysfunctional behaviors. Interventions should aim at altering the child's negative expectations about the world and promoting positive, stable attachments to loving caregivers. Such strategies should amplify the child's remaining resiliency and recuperative powers on the road to healthier functioning.

EPILOGUE

When it comes to the lives of seriously troubled children, I have great faith in the healing power of the family--foster or adoptive. True, these youngsters can erect barriers against those families who would attempt to reach them and to provide that healing power--the curative and unique impact that only a family can offer. When the child's walls go up, the family is often left on the outside. Unconventional strategies may help the walls come tumbling down so that the family may apply the soothing balm of structure, love and understanding to the child's emotional wounds.

After enough healing time within good foster and adoptive homes (and with the support of other treatment team members), dramatic positive changes may occur in the child. Where once there was mistrust of caregivers and suspicion toward potential attachment figures, these children learn faith in others and acceptance of healthier human bonds. Where children once acted-out in distressing ways, they eventually learn to vocalize how they feel and what they want and need. Where a feeling of powerlessness, worthlessness and victimization permeated their every act, there now grows a sense of interpersonal strength, individual worth and assertive, appropriate self-protection.

Unfortunately, we are losing foster homes and prospective adoptive families left and right. Much effort is directed at recruiting good homes, but insufficient resources are aimed at retaining willing families. While foster and adoptive parents are crucial to successful intervention with disturbed children, they are rarely acknowledged as such. As mentioned before, foster and adoptive families are an endangered species.

In the preface of this book we asked about the shrinking numbers of foster and adoptive families. Three factors related to the shrinkage were mentioned:

> 1) the severity of disturbance in today's foster and adoptive children;
>
> 2) inadequate preparation and follow-up support to parents; and

3) the failure to equip foster and adoptive parents with practical therapeutic strategies for dealing with serious problem behaviors.

Here are some additional reasons that good foster and adoptive families are vanishing:

1) We give foster and adoptive parents a disturbed child, and then later misperceive that they might be the source of the child's disturbance (cf. section on "Refrigerator Mother");

2) We exclude these families from the "treatment team", though they are the individuals who often know the children best and who have the greatest therapeutic impact on them;

3) In the case of foster parents, they are given most of the responsibility and none of the authority for the child;

4) Foster parents are asked to become intimately involved with a child, yet are chastised if they grow attached or become "overly zealous advocates" for the child;

5) We expect foster and adoptive families to treat children who may need psychiatric hospital or residential care, yet we do not adequately prepare and support them to provide such intensive services; and

6) We furnish little or no respite care to allow foster and adoptive parents time for re-fueling.

Finally, in closing, my hope is that this book in some small way will help foster and adoptive parents in their efforts to reach disturbed children with their special healing power.

REFERENCES AND RECOMMENDED READING

Ainsworth, Mary D. Salter; Blehar, Mary; Waters, Everett; and Wall, Sally. *Patterns of Attachment: A Psychological Study of the Strange Situation.* New Jersey: Lawrence Erlbaum Associates, 1978.

Ambert, Anne-Marie. *The Effect of Children on Parents.* Binghamton, NY: Haworth Press, 1992.

Barkley, Russell. *Attention-Deficit Hyperactivity Disorder: A Handbook for Diagnosis and Treatment.* New York: Guilford, 1990.

Bowlby, John. *Attachment and Loss. Volume II: Separation.* New York: Basic Books, 1973.

Delaney, Richard J. *Fostering Changes: Treating Attachment-Disordered Foster Children.* Ft. Collins, CO: Walter J. Corbett, 1991.

Delaney, Richard J. and Kunstal, Frank R. *Troubled Transplants: Unconventional Strategies for Healing Disturbed Foster and Adoptive Children.* Portland, Maine. University of Southern Maine, 1993.

Fahlberg, Vera I. *A Child's Journey Through Placement.* Indianapolis, IN: Perspectives Press, 1991.

Farber, Ellen and Egeland, Byron. "Invulnerability among Abused and Neglected Children," In E. James Anthony and Bertram J. Cohler (Eds.) *The Invulnerable Child.* New York: Guilford Press, 1987.

Greenspan, Stanley and Greenspan, Nancy Thorndike. *First Feelings: Milestones in the Emotional Development of Your Baby.* New York: Penguin Books, 1985.

Murphy, L.B., and Moriarity, A. *Vulnerability, Coping and Growth: From Infancy to Adolescence.* New Haven, CT: Yale University Press, 1976.

Sakheim, George A. and Osborn, Elizabeth. *Firesetting Children: Risk Assessment and Treatment.* Washington, D.C.: CWLA, 1994.

Speltz, Matthew L. "The Treatment of Preschool Conduct Problems: An Integration of Behavioral and Attachment Concepts," In Mark T. Greenberg; Dante Cicchetti; and E. Mark Cummings (Eds.) *Attachment in the Preschool Years.* Chicago: University of Chicago Press, 1990.